C000122295

ARTICLE 1

THE STUDY OF

BREATHING & AIR SUPPORT IN SINGING

(A PROVEN NEW APPROACH)

BY

PATRICK C. K. YAM

ISBN: 9781726638500

BWB PUBLISHING

COPYRIGHT

Copyright © 2018 by Patrick C.K. Yam. All rights reserved worldwide. No part of this publication may be replicated, redistributed, or given away in any form without the prior written consent of the author/publisher or the terms relayed herein.

Contents

PREFACE

THE *Book of Singing* contains many intriguing concepts, recognized singing procedures, and techniques that can use to improve one's singing. It has been said that to become the master of a subject one has to dedicate at least ten years of consistent learning and practice and for those who show less dedication will only become the followers of masters. *The Book of Singing* offers to those who are willing to learn the necessary skills to achieve success in singing, but most of all, the book helps to improve singing so that the participants can sing naturally and freely. *The Book of Singing*, however, can not provide fame and wealth to its readers; it is merely a book to help those with interest in singing and entertaining, and perhaps, one day its readers can enrich the lives of many others who are also interested in singing, entertaining, sharing, and inspiring others. However, nothing can realize without an affordable book. The idea of affordability has prompted the writer to divide and excerpt materials from the *Book of Singing* into manageable and affordable sizes of individual articles - one course, one article, one specific subject, without having to pay the full price of the entire book - readers can now read the subjects of their choice at affordable prices.

INTRODUCTION

AIR is the sole element that is responsible for making a vocal sound. Air energizes the vocal cords to vibrate intensively enough to produce sound. The source of air to create sound is vitally important. The question of where and how the air comes from to do the job will determine the quality of the sound produced. The breathing that supports the singing (aka Air Support) is the focus of this article.

EXCELLENT air support is essential to singing. There are many cases of supposedly right singing turn terrible for reasons of wrong and inaccurate breathing influences. Part 1 of this article spells out some of these influences that are causing adverse impacts on what is supposed to be a good singing.

GOOD singing comes from proper breathing techniques. A proper breathing technique is a natural flow technique with natural respiration that blends in well with singing. This article helps the readers to choose a natural breathing technique to practice and use as the air support technique for singing. An air support technique that is known as the "One-Step Breathing Technique (OSBT)" is opted to compare with the other breathing techniques for its effectiveness and limitations for use in singing. Later, the "One-Step Breathing Technique (OSBT)" will be incorporated with the "Yam's One-Step Breathing And Singing Technique (YOSBST) to sing.

THE next publication: Article 2 "The Study of Voices in Singing" will give further validity of the "One-Step Breathing Technique" to achieve optimum results by applying it to varies singing techniques in the diverse genre of singing.

Part 1 – Stamp Out Those Myths & Bad Habits

INEFFECTIVE AIR SUPPORTING TECHNIQUES

AIR support has been one of the most misunderstood topics in singing. The shortfalls are likely due to people's own false beliefs, myths, inaccurate and inferior techniques, and lastly but not least, improper training.

INEXPERIENCED singers are often used improper and artificial air support techniques in their singing. Most of these techniques usually require a gush of air injected into the lungs, then ejected as one sings. Air support in such a way is artificial, and forceful, and is not conducive to good singing - this practice of air support is often detrimental to one's voice, health, and can cause unnecessary exhaustion.

INCLUDED in this section are some of the inaccurate breathing techniques which are currently in circulation among the singing communities. If anyone is using the so-called "BAD" techniques, disregard them and start to do it "RIGHT" by using functional techniques. We should always be vigilant of what is taught and from whom we are learning. Teachers and coaches will find the materials in this article useful to use as references in their teaching, and the information is an excellent source to defend against those improper and incorrect practices.

The following list shows some examples of "BAD" and "MYTHS breathing techniques that are in circulation and practice:

"BAD" & "MYTHS" Breathing Techniques

X   Belly-Pushing Technique

X   Rib-Cage-Raising Technique

X   Traditional Way

X   Diaphragm-Pumping Technique

X   Air-Charged-Up Technique

X   Belly-Button-Tucking Technique (aka Dan Tian)

X   Crazy Chair-Lifting Mythos

BELLY-PUSHING TECHNIQUE

THE belly pushing method requires participants to take a long deep breath pushing out the belly, hold and lock it in a position while they sing. It was shocking to learn that many participants had acquired this technique from their teacher who failed to give an acceptable explanation. Pushing down and holding the belly in a position can lock the diaphragm muscles limiting its movements. Furthermore, most of the functions required for respiration will stop acting correctly. Singing in such a way could hurt the vocal cords – immobility of the diaphragm muscles will affect the supply of air for lubrication and interfere with vocal cords vibration. Some teachers call this technique as "shifting the stomach technique," which evidently will not work. The simple rule for a good air support never has to lock any muscles that are required to move air back and forth within the respiratory system to produce sound.

Ribcage-Raising Technique

THIS technique originates from an old belief that if one were to expand the ribcage by raising it during breathing, one could take more air into the lungs. No doubt, when the ribcage is out of the way a bit, the lungs can house more breath for the singing. However, why does one need copious air to sing in the first place? Isn't having just "enough" air to sing is sufficient? The answer is an assenting "yes." There is no need to having a huge reservoir of air made ready to sing, besides more air will muffle the sound and it…and it does! Notably, one will lose the rhythms of music - one will never "catch up" with the music because the movements of the ribcage will slow the breathing process. Furthermore, jerking the ribcage back and forth will make the sound fluctuated, and that is not acceptable. Today, a better technique is used to replace this improper technique of ribcage movement, and it is the "One-Step Breathing and Singing Technique" which is the focus of this article.

DIAPHRAGM-PUMPING TECHNIQUE

WHEN we sing, our diaphragm moves naturally and correspondingly to the needs of our singing. However, if we were to pump our diaphragm with the intention to fetch air to sing, we are tampering with the movements of the diaphragm. Pumping the diaphragm does not mean that we will have a better air supply for the singing. The result usually ends with the calamity that can lead to the loss of voice, inferior tone quality, exhaustion, and frustration. These are just a few examples of the ravagement that diaphragm pumping can cause, and therefore, it is not advisable to use. Most misinformed beginners and amateur use this form of air support. Keep in mind that there is no singing that requires the diaphragm to be manipulated in such a way, even in the event of "Belting," that the diaphragm reacts naturally and unintentionally to a sudden surge of air to support the singing, and there is no need for any deliberated actions to make it work. Pumping diaphragm for breath is artificial, pondered and damaging, do not use this technique to breathe in singing.

TRADITIONAL WAY

AMONG the many ways of air support, the Traditional Method makes a little more sense in fulfilling the functions of air support, and it has been the backbone of the mainstream teaching for many years, even today. The Traditional Method prompts the intake of air to fill the lungs before any singing begins – it is the idea of always having air in our system to sing. Theoretically, this practice makes some sense; however, in real tight situations when we are singing a fast-paced song, we do not have time to catch our breath, and we shall find ourselves behind in timing as we try to breathe to match the rhythm of the song. With this technique, agilely air replenishing is a significant problem – the harder we work, the worst it becomes as we gasp and gulp for air to catch up with the music. That is why this air-supporting technique is not considered to be the first choice to use for singing.

AIR-CHARGED-UP TECHNIQUE

THE air-charged-up technique is the craziest and ludicrous techniques, and it was made aware by a former student of a singing coach in town. The student was asked to state the number of songs that she would sing in an upcoming performance. She acknowledged that she would sing a total of three songs. She was then given a CD with an unknown song and was told to sing along in repetition for an hour for a total of $30. This procedure was supposed to help her to store enough air for three songs that she would be singing at the performance. The CD was only good for three songs, at the cost of $10 per song. If she were to sing more songs, more money would be required for a longer CD to make it work. The strangest thing, though, was that this so-called "charged-up" procedure would only last for one week or until the completion of the intended performance, whichever came first. Then everything would dissipate, and another recharge would require to store more air in her for the next round.

DON'T laugh! This singing coach owns a good-sized luxury studio in town and has no shortage of believers. Everyone should always be aware of a scam like this, and for sure this method will never work for any style of singing.

BELLY-BUTTON-TUCKING TECHNIQUE (aka DAN TIAN)

THIS method is believed to have been used mostly by the Chinese singing communities, and it has also been the old-school teaching for centuries and is still modestly used by many amateur singers today. "Dan Tian," is a small area, believed to be located around the abdomen area at a short distance above or below (depending on whom you talk to) the belly button. The Dan Tianers, those who use the Dan Tian method, believed that by pushing into the spot of Dan Tian will lift the diaphragm helping it to gush air upward to support the singing. However, the drawback of this breathing method is that air is artificially manipulated in and out of the respiratory system, and that air has to be inhaled rapidly to fill the lungs only to get pushed back quickly. By applying the Dian Tian, and in many cases, the severe tucking and prolonged holding of the abdominal muscles trying to stabilize the air flow, is detrimental to one's vocal health and undoubtedly has no significant benefit to singing.

TODAY, this form of air support is still in use, especially among beginners and intermediate singers who have been taught by friends with little knowledge in singing, and also by many teachers who have learned it in the same way and are now passing down the skills to their students. The advice is to avoid using this technique and any other ones that required a need to fiddle with the natural respiration process.

THE CRAZY CHAIR-LIFTING MYTHOS

THIS myth is among the top most absurd teachings offered to students; it demands students to lift a chair and walk or run with it as they sing. The teacher believes that this practice can help to draw air in and out to supply the singing. It is absurd! Don't ever believe it! Leave the site before the lesson is over.

A word of advice when choosing an air-supporting technique for singing: be aware of the source of information, demand a reasonable explanation, even from the teacher. Reject any teaching that does not make sense. Correct breathing technique will always allow one to sing effortlessly, freely, comfortably and indubitably can apply to all styles of singing; incorrect breathing technique will do just the opposite.

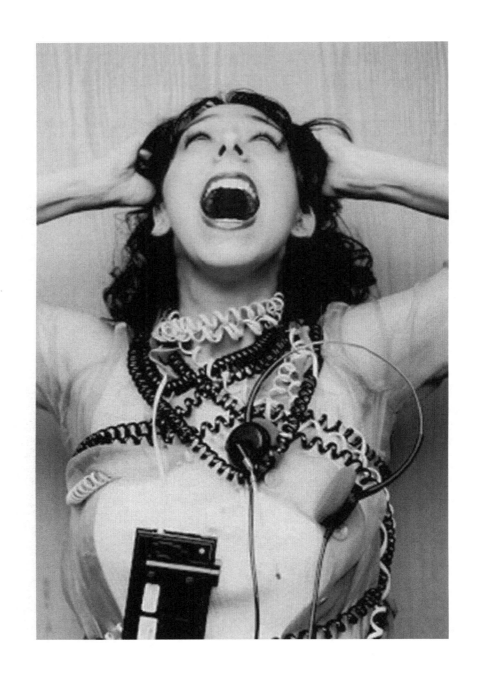

DON'T SING IN CRISIS

PART 2 - LEARN THE ONLY AIR SUPPORT TECHNIQUE THAT ONE EVER NEEDS

THE BASIC CONCEPT OF AIR SUPPORT

When we talk or sing, the majority of the air is inhaled through the mouth, and only a small fraction of air is channeled through the nose. When we exhale, most air is vented out (dissipated) through the sound we made with a small amount escaping through the nose, and this phenomenon is perfectly natural. Experience it when you speak and try it in your singing, and you will find that singing is using the same and identical inhale-exhale process as we talk.

THE physiological attributes of the human inhale and exhale process is not difficult to understand; however, the application of it to support sound production is a little challenging.

BREATHING air (inhale) into the lungs will make the lungs expand pushing the diaphragm downward as illustrated in Diagram D1. Inhale completes half of the breathing process; the other half of the process is when the lungs expel the air from the inside to equate the atmospheric pressure. Diagram D2 - Exhale, shows how the diaphragm moves up, compressing the lungs to empty the air content and with that, completes the cycle of inhaling and exhaling. A discussion of how the process initiates sound for singing will be covered in the next section of this article. For now, think of air as fuel, vocal cords as the engine of a vehicle, and sound as the power which is the derivative of fuel and the engine. The better we can manage the fuel for the engine, the more power we will get. On the same token, the more we know how to handle the air to support our singing, the better the sound will be. We always breathe in through our nose (inhale) and breathe out (exhale) through our nose naturally. This action is so natural that we do not have to learn it; we are born with it. Another innate habit, though, is not so obvious, it is the way we inhale and exhale is different when we talk. Talking requires air to breathe through the mouth where the majority of the air is inhaled, allowing only a small fraction of air to be taken in through the nose and it is utterly natural. When it comes to exhaling, air is breathed out automatically following through the sound we produce. The process applies to all vocal sounds that we make including singing. It is entirely healthy and habitually natural.

DIAGRAM D1

DURING INHALATION

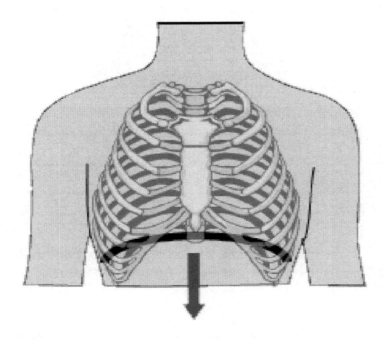

DIAPHRAGM MOVES DOWNWARD AS THE LUNGS FILL WITH AIR

DIAGRAM D2

DURING EXHALATION

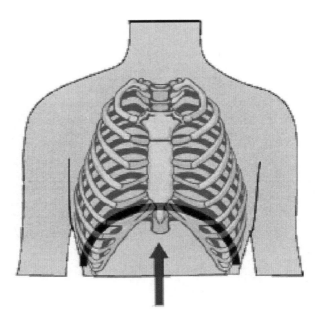

DIAPHRAGM MOVES UPWARD AS THE AIR IS RELEASED

The 9 Vital Functions of Air Support In Singing

AIR in singing is as crucial as fuel to a vehicle, without it there will be nothing to drive our vocal cords, which is comparable to the engine of a vehicle. Knowing the functions of air to sing are vital to give the air a direction and a proper route to do its job. The functions of air are therefore worthy to let known of their valuable contributions.

There are nine functions of air support to singing:

1. Air is needed to keep our body in check allowing any actions that require its presence to be able to carry out their tasks and singing is one of those actions that require air input to make it work.

2. Air is needed to generate sound - whenever air moves through the vocal cords, it causes the vocal cords to vibrate, and it is the vibration of the vocal cords that give out the sound.

3. Air provides cooling (as a lubricant) to the vocal cords, and if without air, nodules and polyps will form.

4. Air carries sound to different acoustic points inside our body. Discussion of this function is not within the scope of this article. An analysis of this function will be in Article 2: "The Study of Voices in Singing."

5. Air helps to sustain sound which means sound can have extra time to reach various locations in the body to get acoustic enhancements, and the extended time gained also allows some lengthy notes a chance to complete the course of duration.

6. Air plays an important role to express emotions and improve pitching.

7. Air helps to link lyrics and notes which makes the singing suave and flowing, and it is known as singing in the style of "legato," which produces a deeper feel. The non-continuous flow of air makes a song sounds more like in "staccato" giving the song a sway effect.

8. Air generates pressure inside the mouth, which helps to stabilize the sound.

9. Air brings sound into different regions inside the body such as: into the head cavity for high notes giving rise to head sound also known as the head voice, and the low notes are directed into the chest cavity forming chest sound known as the chest voice. The sound that comes through these regions of the body holds a unique clarity sound quality known as resonance.

THESE functions bring the meaning and purpose of air support, and when we use them correctly, there will be a definite improvement in the voice quality. The combination of active air support and a beautiful voice are critical to a memorable singing performance.

MANY singers assume that singing should implicate the need to use abundant of air to make it work. This belief provokes them to inhale excessively for every note they pitch, and even more so with notes that are at the extremities of the scales. In reality, there is no need to breathe in more air than needed for any notes at any given time. Excessive inhaling is not the correct way to breathe. It will lead to many shortfalls such as loss in tone quality, muffle sound and usually resulted in causing erroneous rhythm in singing. A precise amount of air is plenty to sing any songs of any style, and it is advisable not to breathe in advance before singing – prematurely taking in the air will cause air support unmanageable, so don't do it!

> Once committed to using small breathings to sing, we shall notice a considerable improvement in the way we sing. Later, our singing will advance prominently with the use of the "One-Step Breathing Technique."

IN order to master the use of just the precise volume of air to sing, we have to learn to start with using one shot of air for every note that we sing. This "one-breath-one-note" procedure is the basic concept of breathing in singing. Try to sing a few notes in such a way then stop. Is there any feeling of having just enough air for every note that we sing? This procedure leads us to find the proper air supporting technique that satisfies the nine functions of air support. Any other techniques that are overly or underly supply air will lead to numerous deficiencies entailing poor sound production.

LATER in the article, we shall find out more about this technique and how the "One-Step Breathing and Singing" method can change the way we sing.

TESTING THE LIMITS OF AIR SUPPORT

LET us review the functions of air support,

1.   Air is needed to keep our body in check allowing any actions that require its presence to be able to carry out their tasks and singing is one of those actions that require air input to make it work.

2.   Air is needed to generate sound - whenever air moves through the vocal cords, it causes the vocal cords to vibrate, and it is the vibration of the vocal cords that give out the sound.

3.   Air provides cooling (as a lubricant) to the vocal cords, and if without air, nodules and polyps will form.

4.   Air carries sound to different acoustic points inside our body. Discussion of this function is not within the scope of this article. An analysis of this function will be in Article 2: "The Study of Voices in Singing."

5.   Air helps to sustain sound which means sound can have extra time to reach various locations in the body to get an acoustic enhancement, and the extended time gained also allows some lengthy notes a chance to complete the course of duration.

6.   Air plays an important role to express emotions and improve pitching.

7.   Air helps to link lyrics and notes which makes the singing suave and flowing, and it is known as singing in the style of "legato," which produces a deeper feel. The non-continuous flow of air makes a song sounds more like in "staccato" giving the song a sway effect.

8.   Air generates pressure inside the mouth, which helps to stabilize the sound.

9.   Air brings sound into different regions inside the body such as: into the head cavity for high notes giving rise to head sound also known as the head voice, and the low notes are directed into the chest cavity forming chest sound known as the chest voice. The sound that comes through these regions of the body holds a unique clarity sound quality known as resonance.

THE ideal amount of air intake to make these functions work correctly is a balancing act. If inhaling too much or too little air, some features of the air support will not work correctly. Ineffective air support will impede the process of making good sound – one of the factors responsible for sounding "bad" is the fluctuation of air through abnormal respiration during singing. The erratic vibration caused by the air fluctuation also stress out the vocal cords.

LET us take a closer look at why are so many individuals with difficulty to breathe in singing. It can be explained in the way that we breathe, in other words, if we breathe incorrectly, we are destined to run into problems and limitations of the accountable breathing technique.

THE following are five breathing procedures which have issues when used in breathing. All of these procedures have their limitations and singers should avoid using them.

BREATHING PROCEDURES WITH LIMITATIONS

PROCEDURE 1. Inhale through the nose before singing.

PROCEDURE 2. Inhale through the mouth before singing.

PROCEDURE 3. Inhale through the nose and mouth before singing.

PROCEDURE 4. Inhale and then expel air by pressing the stomach to force it out to extract the sound.

PROCEDURE 5. Inhale deeply to ensure a vast supply of air in the storage for the singing.

THE LIMITATIONS

PROCEDURE 1 – 3   THE best way to explore the validity of these procedures is by looking at ourselves in a mirror while we are doing it. Take a quick deep breath, and we shall see our head jerks backward, and at the same instant, the eyes will also open widely. It is because we are bringing in additional air to the previously air-filled lungs without appropriately emptying the content - the air inside the lungs will stop extra air to enter. However, if we were to release the air ahead in an attempt to take in more of it, we shall lose the rhythm of the music. Air and sound must happen at precisely the same time as implied in the One-Step Breathing Technique to become efficient, and to fulfill the nine functions of air support.

> ## Go Natural
>
> Always use a technique that is closely related to our natural and habitual movements. Avoid any artificial and dead-end skills which lead to problems.

PROCEDURE 4   THIS procedure demands an external force to manipulation the abdomen muscles to administer the air supply. This practice contradicts the natural approach and inevitably causing major setback and disappointment among those who use it.

PROCEDURE 5   THE practice of deep breathing has no place in singing. The more air we breathe, the harder we can find our voice.

BREATHING PROCEDURES WITHOUT LIMITATIONS: THE ONE-STEP BREATHING TECHNIQUE

THERE is a better way to control breathing as we sing. The One-Step Breathing Technique is identified to resemble and follow the way we usually breathe when we talk. When we sing with the One-Step Breathing Technique, we feel so much relax and have more control of singing. The natural way of it has minimized all possible limitations that are holding back our singing. For simplicity, we shall abbreviate the One-Step Breathing Technique as OSBT, and either one will be addressed in this article interchangeably.

OSBT focuses on how participants can make sound with the natural support of air. The question of why air supporting for singing so complexed and yet can be so comfortable in talking must be answered. Two important things to remember when choosing air support: first, find out the source of it – natural or artificial, second, how to use it? The choice of air support must choose from techniques using natural breathing – just as we breathe and talk. To use it properly, we must also know how we should manage to use it – unfortunately, some of us have developed a hoarse voice regardless of using natural breathing. The management of voice is, therefore, a vital topic which we shall discuss thoroughly in the subsequent article "The Study of Voices in Singing."

THE ONE-STEP BREATHING & SINGING TECHNIQUE

GOOD singing requires good air support, and this is why we should use the One-step Breathing Technique (OSBT). OSBT gives us all the air we need to sing correctly and can fulfill all the functions of air support. Let us review some tidbits of excellent air support which should meet the following requirements:

- ⬚   Gives precisely the amount of air to support as we sing.

- ⬚   Provides efficient air flow to keep the rhythm of the music.

- ⬚   Provides a natural and efficient way to sing.

- ⬚   Directs flow to reach various acoustic points for enhancement.

- ⬚   Allow the vocal cords to cool effectively.

- ⬚   Provides pitching with a precise proportionate of air.

- ⬚   Maintains proper pressure to give a steady flow of sound and tones.

- ⬚   Gives excellent support for an air surge, for example, in the event of "Belting."

- ⬚   Gives singing well flexible support.

WE can now assess any air support techniques based on this 9-point evaluation system. The 9-point evaluation of air support is the minimum requirements to validate and to qualify air supporting procedures. The One-Step Breathing Technique is the only technique with immaculate procedures to score the highest among all the other air supporting procedures. Next, we shall make use of the One-Step Breathing Technique to sing.

How To Make Use Of The One-Step Air Support Technique To Sing

THERE are two steps involved to get us into the routine of making the one-step air support Technique to work effectively:

THE FIRST STEP: Develop a natural air flow for singing.

THE SECOND STEP: Train to breathe to sing just as we speak.

Develop A Natural Flow Of Air For Singing – [The First Step]

The inward flow of air helps to sustain notes which can be mixed at various acoustic points inside the mouth cavity to obtain acoustic enhancement before it reaches the audience.

WE have experienced the natural flow of air since the day we were born – we inhale and exhale naturally without having to worry about how it is done. Every breath of respiration is a clockwork precision, and we do it naturally. Then why do we have to uncover this instinct, innate, natural breathing? It is because many of us do not become aware that we can use the same breathing method for almost all vocal activities, and singing is among one of them. All oral communications such as talking, chitchatting, confabbing are using the same air support found in natural breathing.

LET'S focused on bringing in the air through normal breathing to support our singing. Have we ever noticed we are using our mouth to breathe when we talk? Are we aware that air starts to connect to the sound as soon as we vocalize? Are we also aware that we are breathing in the air instead of breathing out the air when we vocalize? Yes, it is all true that we are breathing in air through the mouth and the air will, instantly, connect with any sound that we make, for example, in talking or singing. We can further realize it by talking and singing in a louder and softer voice, and the result will be the same, that is, we always breathe in through the mouth. The next step is to train to develop muscles to remember so that we can do it every time in the same way.

ALTHOUGH it is evident that the use of natural air support is best for singing, many skeptics believe that singing is relatively different from talking because, in singing, there is the need to pitch all the notes at different values, and furthermore, singing is mostly in a louder voice than talking. Therefore, singing should demand more air to make it work – subsequently, many versions of air support techniques emerged.

THE success of using natural air support to sing depends on two factors – 1. Mindset, and 2. Frequent practice.

MINDSET is the determination to do what we think is right. Doing the right thing might imply that we have to change anything that we have been doing wrong – we need the courage to change our mind to start doing things right. Changing our mind will be challenging, we must, therefore, be willing to accept changes – we must permit ourselves to change, and a will to become better.

TRAINING is next on the agenda to apply the natural air support technique (OSBT) to singing. The first step of the training requires us to breathe through the mouth when we sing. It is essential that we must sing and inhale at precisely the same moment to make it work. To do it correctly, we shall try to do a "ha," making sure that we are taking in just a tiny shot of air for it. Remember, it is nothing new here because we have been doing it all the time in speaking. There is a similarity in singing which employs the same breathing technique as in speaking, and that is, to sing and inhale at the same time through the mouth, and it is natural. There are two things to remember here: first, in talking and singing, we inhale, not exhale, at vocalization. Second, a small, natural steady flow of air at inhaling is all that is required to initiate and sustain the sound. Any forced air by any means will ruin the natural breathing process associated with the technique.

No one should have any problem using natural air support for the singing.

Physical preparation: practice singing in the way we talk and breathe until we are good at it.

Mental preparation: permit ourselves to use the technique.

A Mini Summary – The First Step

[The First Step]

1   Inhale using the mouth only.
2   Inhale while making a sound.
3   Do not fill the lungs in advance
     before singing.
4   Sing at inhaling, not at exhaling.
5   Do it naturally, do not force air
     into the lungs or likewise, out
     from the lungs.

TRAIN TO BREATHE AND SING IN THE WAY THAT IS USED TO TALK – [THE SECOND STEP]

IF we have guessed right, we know we have to take in the air when we sing. That is, breathe and sing at the same time. Singing and breathing have to happen precisely together. This process happens every time we talk; we breathe and speak at the same time, and it is so natural that we are probably not aware of it.

To make the One-Step Air Support work for us, we must believe that we can apply the way we talk to singing. Now try to say a few words, or perhaps a few sentences, and observe, paying attention to see if we are moving the air outward (blowing out) or moving the air inward (sucking in) when we talk. It is noteworthy to realize that air is not blowing out but pulling in when we talk. Say "hi" a few times. Now say it louder. Are we convinced? If the sound comes out as a "whisper," we are blowing out air, and "whispering" is occasionally used in singing.

LET'S practice it on singing. Sing a few words or sentences from a song that we know. Sing one word at a time without blowing out air, but keep it inside our mouth, or better still, keep it at the back of our throat. Now *imagine* that we are sucking in the "*Sound*" of each word, not air, and as we do that, air will automatically draw inward simultaneously with the sound. Repeat the procedure by doing it with more songs. Keep practicing until our muscles can remember.

IMPORTANT: Always pick the songs that we know to practice, this way we do not have to worry about other things such as tunes, and lyrics. The use of this technique is suitable for any styles of singing, and it is beneficial to those who use it for their songs, because,

1) It is natural, and we are using the same breathing process to vocalize daily. Therefore, it is easy to comprehend.

2) It only requires a small, precise volume of air to work keeping excessive breathing at bay.

3) Air is always replenished rather than depleted. Air is drawn in to support the singing instead of blown out depleting the air supply.

4) It enhances the sound at different acoustic points inside the mouth.

5) Sound can effectively reach at the respective registers for resonance.

6) It allows proper airflow for pitching.

7) It gives sufficient air in the case of sudden air surging.

8) Air Keeps the vocal cords in the downward position. Therefore, less stress for the vocal cords.

9) It provides flexible sound volume

SINGING is very much like talking when comes to using air supply, and these are just some of the benefits when we use natural air support (OSBT). Don't worry if we are not able to fully understand the benefits that come with this technique. Some points that we mention here are related to the production of the vocal sound which we will learn in the subsequent articles. In the meantime, focus on the next few sections to determine how the technique of natural air support can benefit us.

NEXT, let us explore the concept of the "One-Step Breathing Technique," which is closely related to natural breathing. However, first, more facts: many of us have already known, and all of us have experienced, "Natural Breathing," but less of us make use of it as the singing tool. In reality, singing with natural breathing is the best procedure ever used - it requires no artificial means to recruit air. Many singing individuals, including some teachers, have believed that singing should require some special breathing procedures - the use of muscles to move air back and forth, to and from, the lungs. The original of such beliefs is unknown, but inevitably, have caused many sorrows and disappointments. Yes, these sorts of ideas are fallacies, and all artificial practices must not be encouraged.

THE meaning of natural air support is merely meaning to breathe without having to rely on any other means of support, or intervention by anything, anyone, or any self. Natural air support is automatic and stand-alone, and it can help us to craft our voice into beautiful singing.

A MINI SUMMARY – THE SECOND STEP

[The Second Step]

1. Practice singing the songs that we know.
2. Sing at inhaling.
3. Imagine we are drawing sound as we inhale.
4. Start with one note at a time, then proceed to sing more notes.
5. Keep the air and sound at the back of the throat for the duration of the notes.
6. Practice until it anchors into the muscles to achieve lasting memory.

MORE ON NATURAL BREATHING & SINGING

QUESTION:

Ever wonder what has happened to the air that we inhaled during singing? Where does it go?

ANSWER:

The air is quickly and naturally dissipated through the sound we produced.

AS we communicate, we are most likely unaware that we are breathing, and we enunciate words spontaneously; we do not have to be aware of how and when we breathe and talk at the same time; it just happens.

INTERESTINGLY, we seldom aware that the air we breathe as we vocalize is routinely pulled in through our mouth. Activities such as talking and singing, are following the same natural breathing. It is this pulled-in action that caused the flow of air downward to vibrate the vocal cords which give off the sound.

MANY fail to sing well because they have neglected to make use of the fundamental instinct of natural breathing to sing. Without it, the singing is unnatural and constrained.

REVIEW

SINGING uses natural breathing in the same way as all vocalization does such as talking, laughing, crying, shouting. The characteristic of natural breathing is that it does not require any forced air to make it work.

"TO SING PROPERLY, WE MUST BREATHE IN THE SAME WAY AS WE SPEAK."

To maximize the singing quality, be sure to sing at inhaling and NEVER sing at exhaling.

THE CONCEPT OF THE ONE-STEP BREATHING TECHNIQUE

The One-Step Breathing Technique is closely tied to natural breathing, and using it correctly will make our singing natural. The One-Step Breathing Technique is easy to understand and simple to use – we can breathe and sing at the same time. It is the only air support that we should use for singing. The natural breathing process requires no external force and internal manipulation to make a sound, and that is why we have the freedom to sing without impediment. Let us look at how we can apply it to singing.

FIRST, let us find out how air supports vocalization such as talking, laughing, shouting, crying. When we speak, we take in air, and when we talk faster, we take in more air. It is so natural, automatic, and we do it subconsciously - we do not even notice how much air we are taking in to make a sound – we just do it. Whenever we vocalize, we inhale by drawing air inward (sucking in air) to vibrate the vocal cords to generate sound. We exhale through the dissipation of the sound, and the speed of air that is released is almost as quickly as the intake. The cycle of inhaling and exhaling will start again with the production of the next sound.

The following two steps lead us to find out more about sound making with natural breathing:

Step 1:   Try to inhale and exhale through the mouth without making any sound. Once we feel the air is rushing in through the mouth, proceed to Step 2.

Step 2:   Talk, sing or yell while Inhaling air through the mouth. We shall do it a few times to realize that the sound we make and the air that supports it happen at precisely the same time. We shall do more talking, yelling, and shouting, or by any means of breaking silence, and the results will remain the same – the air that we breathe in naturally will always support the sound we produce. Once we understand it, proceed to the next section to learn to sing with the One-Step Breathing Technique.

USING THE ONE-STEP BREATHING TECHNIQUE (OSBT) TO SING

SOUND begins when the air we breathe passes through the vocal cords causing them to vibrate. The vibrations produce the sound that makes singing possible.

WE have learned the concept from the previous section referred to as the "One-Step Breathing Technique, in short (OSBT)" is the only breathing technique that can fulfill the requirements of proper air support, and to make it work, we must follow the following specifics:

- Air must be inhaled using the mouth, not by the nose, as we sing. In doing that, air is drawn inward and down towards the vocal cords. The downward draft of air vibrates the vocal cords strongly enough to produce sound.

- Air must be inhaled at the precise moment as soon as we start to sing. In reality, air is always inhaled just a fraction before the initiation of sound. Remember, air causes the vocal cords to vibrate to make a sound. However, if we inhale heavily without making any noise (only breathing), we shall probably find our heads "jerking" backward each time as we inhale. This phenomenon is due to air is forced into the prior air-packed lungs. To do it correctly, initiate sound while bringing in the air. This way we are exhausting the air as soon as it finishes the task of causing the vibration of the vocal cords without having to stack it into the lungs.

- It is recommended that we start with using one breath per note until we are comfortable with the procedure. Proceed to sing more notes with just one breath as we have a grip on it.

- When using OSBT, it is important to note that a small portion of air will ventilate through the nose and it is rightly acceptable.

ADVANTAGES OF USING THE ONE-STEP BREATHING TECHNIQUE (OSBT):

1. There is no need to stop for air, and it is, therefore, easier to keep up with the rhythm of the music.

2. Automatic initiate air to support the singing and the replenishment of air is instinctive.

3. The downward draft of air throws the vocal cords downward, preventing them to uplift which can cause stress on the vocal cords.

4. OSBT performs exceptionally well to use as the air support for singing:

    - Provide sufficient air to sing and for the need of the body.

    - Provide smooth airflow sufficiently for the production of sound.

    - Provide cooling, and lubrication to the vocal cords. OSBT helps to prevent the formation of nodules and polyps.

    Tip:

    In practice, it is recommended that no music be used, at least initially. Therefore, we do not have to worry about the rhythms and the key of the songs.

    - Generate pressure at strategic locations inside the mouth cavity keeping the sound acoustic and resonance in check. Discussion of this function is out of the scope of this article. Article 2: "The Study of Voices in Singing (A Proven New Approach)" will cover this function in detail.

    - Helps to keep the sound inside the mouth to prevent any premature escape through projection – Properly mix sound with acoustic before making it public is always a good practice. There will be more on this subject in the subsequent article.

    - Helps to pitch the notes quickly and accurately.

- Helps to link the lyrics, allowing the sound to resonate smoothly and continuously as in the style of "legato" giving the song a deeper feel. The non-continuous flow of air makes the song sound more like in "staccato," giving the song a sway effect.

- It is natural without the use of forced air.

5. Provide an appropriate amount of air to sing - too much air will ruin the singing, and too little will result in lacking enough breath to carry out the task of supporting.

> Breathing in the air to vibrate the vocal cords to make sound has one "big" advantage – it lowers the position of the vocal cords which helps to expand the range of the voice.

6. OSBT prevents the inhaling and exhaling air to collide when singing. The route of the air follows a path that allows the inhaling air to enter, energizing the vocal cords, and carrying the sound to the appropriate acoustic points and comes out in a one-way route, similar to a vehicle traveling along a cul-de-sac, without collision of the incoming and outgoing traffic.

7. OSBT prevents the lifting of the vocal cords when making a sound. The inhaling air has a downdraft that pushes the vocal cords downward to form an ideal singing position.

FEEL THE TECHNIQUE

As we practice the One-Step Breathing Technique (OSBT), try to feel the sound and the incoming air that support the sound. Try to feel the vibrations of the sound and air contacting the back of our throat, and also try to feel as the sound and air leave the cavity of the mouth. Sing a little louder to maximize the feel. Try to use it on those long-linking notes to feel how sound stays contacted at the back of the mouth cavity and eventually dissipates as the duration of the notes phases out. It is important to note that we are getting these feelings throughout the entire song and for all the songs that we sing.

THE COMPARISON OF OSBT VERSUS OTHER BREATHING TECHNIQUES

OSBT	OTHER TECHNIQUES
1. Natural airflow.	1. Forced air flow.
2. Replenish air automatically.	2. Sing with depleting air.
3. No need to store air.	3. Air is stored for the singing.
4. Sing from inhaled air.	4. Sing from exhausted air.
5. The sound can interact freely at various acoustic points inside the mouth cavity.	5. Project the sound prematurely without proper acoustic mixing.
6. Able to produce a smooth-linking sound for the entire duration of a note.	6. Sound for notes duration is harsh and bleak.
7. Able to keep up with the rhythm of the music.	7. Challenging to keep up the rhythm of the music.
8. Position vocal cords naturally as air is inhaling.	8. Vocal cords are pushed upward as air is expelled intensely upward causing immense stress to the vocal cords.
9. Pitching is smooth and precise.	9. Pitching is frequently a hit and miss event.

10. Precision air support
11. No more microphone pops.

10. Inflow and outflow of air are unsteady, resulting in varied and uneven sound.
11. Microphone pops are common occurrences.

AUTHOR'S NOTE:

AS we can see here, the benefits of the "One Step Breathing Technique (OSBT)" have given us many good reasons to adopt it as the most effective breathing tool for singing. The natural traits of OSBT have prompted me to research to try to maximize its potential when used for singing. One of the challenges is to convey the message to the singing communities that natural breathing is excellent for singing as we have been using the same process in our talking. The biggest challenge, though, is to convince the skeptics that natural breathing is effective and efficient. The One-Step Breathing Technique (OSBT) which uses 100% of unforced air to support should be the only breathing technique we should use for singing. However, sadly enough, many of the skeptics have failed to acknowledge the fact, and unwilling to change.

OSBT can significantly improve the voice quality bringing out the timbre of one's voice. It enables us to sing comfortably and deliver the dynamic and emotions of a song effectively. It is all because of a better airflow making use of natural breathing.

I HAVE incorporated the One-Step Breathing Technique (OSBT) and singing into one technique, and I called it "Yam's One-Step Breathing and Singing Technique." In short, "YOSBST (You Sing Best)." YOSBST can be used in every genre of singing. I shall explain this technique further in the next sections. I have structured an easy way to learn YOSBST. Please stay tuned.

YAM'S ONE-STEP BREATHING & SINGING TECHNIQUE (YOSBST)

FOLLOW THESE RULES WHEN USING YAM'S ONE-STEP BREATHING AND SINGING TECHNIQUE (YOSBST)

Follow these rules when using YOSBST

RULES WE MUST FOLLOW TO HAVE YOSBST WORKS BEST FOR US:

When training for YOSBST, we must observe these six rules to benefit from them entirely. The following is a schedule of two phases of the training.

Rule 1
Use the mouth to breathe. Do not use the nose.

Rule 2
Sing at inhaling.

Rule 3
Sing and breathe at the same time.

Rule 4
Breathe deep so that the sound can reach the back of the mouth cavity.

Rule 5
Relax so that the sound and air can dissipate easily and naturally.

Rule 6
Always sing with a narrow opening of the mouth (a small opening), except for articulation.

TRAIN OURSELVES TO USE YAM'S ONE-STEP BREATHING AND SINGING TECHNIQUE (YOSBST)

PHASE 1 – Muscle Training.

PHASE 2 – The Application.

PHASE 1: MUSCLE TRAINING

PHASE 1: MUSCLE TRAINING

Always observe the "6 Rules When Using "YOSBST" mentioned earlier (page 42) when doing the following steps:

Step 1: TAKE a short breath using the mouth and while we are doing it, say "hi" at the same time.

Step 2: SAY "hi" again, but louder this time. We shall find a louder "hi" can make the sound reach further to the back of the mouth cavity.

Step 3: SING a note of choice a few times, from soft to loud. Remember to sing at inhaling.

Step 4: SING a note of choice and continue to sing the note, with the same breath, until we are out. Repeat this step a few times but do not shout as it might put stress on the vocal cords.

Once we have mastered Phase 1, proceed to Phase 2.

PHASE 2: THE APPLICATION

PHASE 2 – THE APPLICATION

Always observe the "6 Rules When Using "YOSBST" mentioned earlier while doing the following steps:

Step 1: SING as many notes as we can in one continuous breath. Do not worry about how many notes we can sing with one single breath. Sing the next set of notes with the next shot of breath. Don't forget to use the mouth to inhale. Don't worry about breaks between phrases - sing right through them!

Step 2: PRACTICE targeting both sound and air to hit the back of the mouth cavity by singing a little louder.

Step 3: SING as many notes as we possibly can, sing until we are out of breath. The idea is to use up any air that we breathe in before acquiring more air to sing. A word of caution, do not try to force out all the air inside the lungs – we do not want to put stress on the vocal cords which could possible lifted when we are trying hard to dump the excess air from the lungs.

Step 4: IF we were running out of breath to sing the next coming notes, pause and continue to sing the next note.

Caution: Do not hyperventilate. Rest often.

Try to get the feeling only, do a few times then stop and rest.

THE THEORY, MORE TRAINING, AND THE PRACTICE OF YAM'S ONE-STEP BREATHING AND SINGING TECHNIQUE (YOSBST)

THE THEORY

A simple intake of air in talking can also be duplicated to use for singing. We all understand that inhaling causes the air to store in our lungs. The stored air, in turn, support the body functions and most of the physical activities that we do. However, vocalization such as talking, singing are the exceptions – the production of vocal sounds does not necessarily require the lungs to store air in advance for subsequent withdrawal. An intake of a modest amount of air at precisely the same time as we vocalize is sufficient to do the job, and it has always been in such a way when we speak. In singing we are following the same route as we speak, that means, we always take in the air as we need it but not before.

THE air intake for singing is a delicate balance - too much or too less air intake will ruin the possibility of good singing. YOSBST provides the solution of having just enough air to sing. YOSBST simplifies the breathing procedure into taking small breaths. To begin learning, we allow ourselves to take one small breath at a time as we sing (do not inhale in advance). The little puff of air is more than enough to sing multiple notes. Take a second breath for the next round of notes and the third for another round and so forth. Continue the process to finish the song. Singing and talking share the same routine of using air support.

FOR those who have difficulty to visualize that breathing and singing can happen simultaneously, imagine swallowing (sucking in) every note. The swallowing action creates a pulling effect of air going into the back of the mouth cavity, and it is this stream of air that causes the vocal cords to vibrate making the production of sound possible.

MORE TRAINING

THE training of the Yam's One-Step Breathing and Singing Technique (YOSBST) is in two stages.

STAGE 1: BASIC TRAINING.

STAGE 2: TARGET TRAINING.

STAGE 1: "Basic Training" is the only topic covered in this article. Stage 2 "Target Training," will be covered in the subsequent article of this series: "The Study of Voices in Singing."

THE theory of YOSBST is simple to understand, and the training of it is accessibly easy. However, it will take time to set into the routine, and most of all, to develop the muscle to remember might take even longer time to achieve. Once it becomes the habit, we shall notice there is a difference in breathing easier, pitching better and sounding better – considerably much better.

The following is a drill to train to use Yam's One-Step Breathing and Singing Technique (YOSBST):

DRILL:

1. SAY a one-syllable word "hi," try to inhale through the mouth as we are saying it. Next, take a breath of air and then say "hi," we shall notice the first "hi" is stronger and with more acoustics, whereas the second "hi" that with air taken in advance appears breathy, dull, and sounds more like a whisper. We shall focus on the way we say the first "hi" in training.

2. NOW say "hi" again or say any one-syllable word of your choice. This time, prolong the sound with a longer duration (Don't forget to say it while taking in air through the mouth). Next, do it again with an even longer duration until we are out of breath. Do we feel the air and sound hitting the back of our throat as we are doing it? If we do not, say the word a little louder until we can feel the sound is touching the back of our mouth or throat. Also, take note that a small amount of air is venting out through our nose as we are doing it, it is perfectly all right to have some air escape through the nose, however majority of the air should dissipate along with the sound through the mouth

3. REPEAT the same drill with a string of one-syllable words. For example, try to say "I love you," and then with a multi-syllable word such as, "Argentina." Say these words with just one shot of breath inhaled through the mouth.

Now let us use a song to practice.

THE PRACTICE

THE time has come to practice Yam's One-Step Breathing and Singing Technique (YOSBST) with a song; pick a song that we know quite well and use it to practice. Try to use a song with less high or low notes, and perhaps, use a simple, slow ballad. Start slowly with one phrase at a time, proceed to do more, and with more songs as we fuse into the technique. Practice, Practice, and more Practice.

IN the subsequent article (The Study of Voices in singing), we shall learn how to use YOSBST to tune the voice. With the use of this technique and with frequent practice, our voice will sound natural and free. A free voice is vibrant, resonant, and fully characterized to reveal one's vocal timbre. However, first, we must fully understand the materials of this article to be able to make good use of the next article, consider this article to be the prerequisite of the subsequent article "The Study of Voices in Singing (A Proven New Approach)."

VALUABLE MUMBO JUMBO

THE concept of Yam's One-Step Breathing and Singing Technique (YOSBST) is not only easy to understand, but the process is natural and it offers a compelling and more natural way to sing. It is the very method that can give us all the air support we need to sing, and at the pace that we want with the precise amount of air. We can use it to sing any style of songs, and It allows us to sing those high and low notes which we thought we would never be able to sing. Also, we shall find a noticeable improvement in the voice.

YAM'S One-Step Breathing and Singing Technique (YOSBST) is a natural process that makes use of one's natural breathing to sing. Every vocalization uses natural breathing - when a baby cries, there is no need to call for air to store ahead, it just happens. Crying and breathing happen at precisely the same time with no need to take in the air in advance. Professional singing has made use of this innate, basic instinct of air support to breath and sing.

There are three groups of singers among us:

GROUP 1: The innate breathers.

GROUP 2: The artificial breathers.

GROUP 3: The lost and the undecided breathers.

GROUP 1 brings out the most naturally produced sound while making use of the opportunity to create sound coherent with the way we talk and breathe.

GROUP 2 artificially adjusts or manipulates the process of breathing, making the sound harsh and forceful (see Part 1 - Stamp Out Those Myths & Bad Habits). If we belong to Group 2, we are strongly advised to take action to learn to breathe correctly - without having to pump air in and out to reach the voice. Artificial breathers need to completely remove any traces of artificial breathing to become proficient singers. Replacing all the deficiencies with the use of a better technique such as YOSBST is a must, and start to sing it right. However, the decision of changing is often influenced by, psychologically, the reluctant to change. The remedy is to permit ourselves to change – to change for the better!

GROUP 3 find themselves puzzled by the many choices of breathing techniques available for singing. This group must be rightly guided to learn correctly. Improper procedures once adapted, are not easy to change. Group 3 can quickly become Group 2 (artificial breathers) if without proper guidance.

Unleash The Air Power

ONCE we have learned Yam's One-Step Breathing and Singing Technique (YOSBST), we can sing songs with greater control of dynamic, rhythm, pitches, and sound. The only thing we shall need now is, perhaps, "confidence." Without confidence, there will be no air support that can keep us intact. One way to build our confidence is to step out of our comfort zone gradually and to expand it by facing different sizes of audiences, and ideally, perform at various venues.

YAM'S one-step Breathing and Singing Technique (YOSBST) allow us to use the precise quantity of air for the singing, and we shall never have to worry about the air supply because it is naturally inhaled and replenished. Now we have the "right stuff" to sing, so unleash the air power in us to make it happen!

Self-Test Questions

THERE are (10) True and False questions and (2) questionnaires to test our knowledge of air support. The self-test questions are for interest only; there is no failure or shame. Answer these questions to the best of your knowledge or guessing. If required, reread the article until you fully understand the materials in this article.

Section 1 - True or False (Answers at the End of the Article)

Q.1   The best air support requires a reasonable and consistent manipulation of all related muscles.

       True   False

Q.2   Filling the lungs with air in advance is the technique to use in singing.

       True   False

Q.3   Air is vital to direct sound to different acoustic regions as one of its supporting functions.

       True   False

Q.4   It is natural to draw air towards the vocal cords so that the air can vibrate the vocal cords to form sound.

         True   False

Q.5   Pumping the diaphragm for air can improve sound dynamics.

         True   False

Q.6   Always make sure there is plenty of air in the lungs ready for the singing.

         True   False

Q.7   Sound should be released through the nose.

         True   False

Q.8   There is no such thing as natural air support.

       True   False

Q.9   Pitching requires adequate air stored in the lungs.

       True   False

Q.10   Yam's One-Step Breathing and Singing technique (YOSBST) can provide precisely the
       right amount of air for singing.

       True   False

SECTION 2 - QUESTIONS & ANSWERS (ANSWERS AT THE END OF THE ARTICLE)

Q.1   Name 4 out of 9 air support functions in singing.

Q. 2   Name at least two advantages of using "One-Step Breathing Technique (OSBT)" to sing.

HEADS UP – WE ARE DOING FINE!

IT is perfectly all right to read the article and the topics of interest more than once to understand the concepts in the article entirely. We must believe in the natural use of air to support singing. It is the only way to train and anchor the technique into the muscles.

WE understand it is not easy to eliminate those bad habits and misbeliefs overnight, but we must strive harder to change in the best way we can, and the earlier, the better. Beginners should always be vigilant when sourcing their teacher and techniques. Do not learn improper techniques or acquire dead-end skills.

ALTHOUGH Yam's One-Step Breathing & Singing Technique (YOSBST) is focused on making use of natural breathing to sing, it might require several drills and practices to incorporate into your singing routine. Allow time to build a good foundation, to form a good habit, and with that, complete the quest for an extraordinary and yet, a natural technique for singing.

PART 4 – A QUICK RECAP OF THE ARTICLE

PART 1:   TALK about some of the myths and incorrect techniques that form bad habits. Disposing of bad habits is always challenging. Myths and inaccurate methods are the main reasons why people have a hard time finding improvements in their singing. All of these myths and wrong practices have problems with their legitimacy and effectiveness. The review and reflection of these techniques are made known to the singing public to aware of their existence, and it is one's choice to change or continue to use them.

PART 2:   IN search of an active air supporting technique to use for singing. The Introduction of the nine vital functions of air support that are essential to good singing. Testing the limits of air support. Things that we must do to have the air support working for us. The meaning of natural air support and how to use it in singing. The concept of the One-Step Breathing Technique as we understand in "speaking." How to use the One-Step Breathing Technique to sing. Introduction of the Yam's One-Step Breathing and Singing Technique (YOSBST), its theory, benefits, training, and practices.

PART 3:   Self-test questions to test the knowledge about air support in singing.

PART 4:   RECAPS OF the article.

PART 5:   SUGGESTION for future reading.

PART 5 - FURTHER READINGS

WHERE DO WE GO FROM HERE?

THIS article focuses on air support which is one of the essential subjects in singing. Air support affects sound which is the next subject of the study. Article 2: "The Study of Voices in Singing (A proven New Approach)," is to study how vocal cords generate sound, how sound can be maximized, refined, and directed. We shall learn to manage air to target different areas to gain acoustic, apply pressure to the voice, and navigate sound to different registers. In short, Article 2 is about sound production, navigation, voice refinement, pitching, the proper use of muscles to sing, and many related topics. Article 2 should be an excellent read to improve the singing.

PUBLICATIONS

SINGING TO SUCCESS

AUTHOR: PATRICK C.K. YAM

PUBLISHER: BWB PUBLISHING, LWB PRESS, LULU PUBLISHING, CREATESPACE

PAPERBACK ISBN: 9781499642612

FORMAT: PAPERBACK, KINDLE

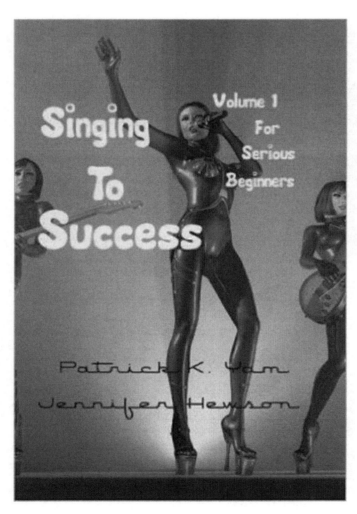

This publication is available at Amazon and bookstore outlets worldwide in printed and e-book formats.

THE STUDY OF BREATHING AND AIR SUPPORT IN SINGING (A PROVEN NEW APPROACH)

AUTHOR: PATRICK C.K. YAM

PUBLISHER: BWB PUBLISHING, LWB PRESS

PAPERBACK: ISBN: 9781726638500

FORMAT: PAPERBACK, KINDLE

THE STUDY OF VOICES IN SINGING (A PROVEN NEW APPROACH)

AUTHOR: PATRICK C.K. YAM

PUBLISHER: BWB PUBLISHING, LWB PRESS

FORMAT: PAPERBACK, KINDLE

DATE OF PUBLICATION: TBA

MOBILIZE YOUR SINGING VOICE

AUTHOR: PATRICK C.K. YAM

PUBLISHER: BWB PUBLISHING, LWB PRESS

FORMAT: PAPERBACK, KINDLE

DATE OF PUBLICATION: TBA

ANSWERS TO SELF-TESTING QUESTIONS

FALSE

Natural air support will never have to manipulate any muscles to make it work. Air support for vocalization such as talking, laughing, and yelling is an excellent example of the natural, innate nature to support without having to tamper with any muscles to make it work.

SECTION 1– Q2 ANSWER

FALSE

There is no need to store air in advance tor any singing.

Um...true!

One of the functions of air support is to carry air to reach different acoustic regions for sound enhancement.

SECTION 1 – Q4 ANSWER

TRUE

It is true that the proper way to access air support is to have air naturally come to us when we sing and when it happens, air is drawn inward (inhale) through the mouth and instantly vibrates the vocal cords to produce sound. The process is perfectly natural.

FALSE

Pumping the diaphragm is the artificial manipulation of the diaphragm muscle which is not advisable. Dynamics of sound are not caused by jouncing the diaphragm.

SECTION 1 – Q6   Answer

FALSE

Jamming more air into wholly or partially filled lungs will cause gasping and in severe cases, choking. The more air gulped, the more pressure from the lungs to expel and reject. Always avoid storing air before we sing. Singing does not require a "large" reservoir of air ready to be deployed. Too much air in the lungs is hard to control and can cause problems when released.

FALSE

When singing, try to let most of the sound out through the mouth allowing only a fraction of sound to seep through the nose – too much sound venting through the nose will cause the sound to become muffled.

SECTION 1 – Q8 ANSWER

FALSE

Only natural air support is recommended to use in singing. Forget any artificial means to make it work.

SECTION 1 – Q9   Answer

FALSE

Pitching does not require to allocate air to store in the lungs to work properly.

SECTION 1 – Q10   ANSWER

TRUE

Q.1   Name 4 out of 9 air support functions in singing.

ANSWER: Choose 4 out of 9 functions listed below:

1.   Air is needed to keep our body in check allowing any actions that require its presence to be able to carry out its task and singing is one of those actions that require air input to make it work.

2.   Air is needed to generate sound - whenever air moves through the vocal cords, it causes the vocal cords to vibrate, and it is the vibration of the vocal cords that give out the sound.

3.   Air provides cooling (as a lubricant) to the vocal cords, and if without air nodules and polyps will form.

4.   Air carries sound to different acoustic points inside our body. Discussion of this function is not within the scope of this article. An analysis of this function will be in Article 2: "The Study of Voices in Singing."

5.   Air helps to sustain sound which means sound can have extra time to reach various locations in the body to get an acoustics enhancement, and the extended time gained also allows some lengthy notes a chance to complete the duration.

6.   Air plays an important role to express emotions and improve pitching.

7.   Air helps to link lyrics and notes which makes the singing suave and flowing, and it is known as singing in the style of "legato," which produces a deeper feel. The non-continuous flow of air makes a song sounds more like in "staccato" giving the song a sway effect.

8.   Air generates pressure inside the mouth, which helps to stabilize the sound.

9.   Air brings sound into different regions inside the body such as: into the head cavity for high notes giving rise to head sound also known as the head voice, and the low notes are directed into the chest cavity forming chest sound known as chest voice. The sound that comes through these regions of the body holds a unique clarity sound quality known as resonance.

Q. 2   Name at least two advantages of using One-Step Breathing Technique (OSBT) to sing.

ANSWER:

1 There is no need to stop for air, and it is, therefore, easier to keep up with the rhythm of the music.

2 Automatic initiate air to support the singing and the replenishment of air is instinctive.

3 The downward draft of air throws the vocal cords downward, preventing them to uplift which can cause stress on the vocal cords.

4 OSBT performs exceptionally well to use as the air support for singing:

- Provide sufficient air to sing and for the need of the body.

- Provide smooth airflow sufficiently for the production of sound.

- Provide cooling, and lubrication to the vocal cords. OSBT helps to prevent the formation of nodules and polyps.

- Generate pressure at strategic locations inside the mouth cavity keeping the sound acoustic and resonance in check. Discussion of this function is out of the scope of this article. Article 2: "The Study of Voices in Singing (A Proven New Approach)" will cover this function in detail.

- Helps to keep the sound inside the mouth to prevent any premature escape through projection – Properly mix sound with acoustic before making it public is always a good practice. There will be more on this subject in the subsequent article.

- Helps to pitch the notes quickly and accurately.

- Helps to link the lyrics, allowing the sound to resonate smoothly and continuously as in the style of "legato" giving the song a deeper feel. The non-continuous flow of air makes the song sound more like in "staccato," giving the song a sway effect.

- It is natural without the use of forced air.

5   Provide an appropriate amount of air to sing - too much air will ruin the singing, and too little will result in lacking enough breath to carry out the task of supporting.

6   OSBT prevents the inhaling and exhaling air to collide when singing. The route of the air follows a path that allows the inhaling air to enter, energizing the vocal cords, and carrying the sound to the appropriate acoustic points and comes out in a one-way route, similar to a vehicle traveling along a cul-de-sac, without collision of the incoming and outgoing traffic.

7   OSBT prevents the lifting of the vocal cords when making a sound. The inhaling air has a downdraft that pushes the vocal cords downward to form an ideal singing position.

NOTES

NOTES

Printed in Great Britain
by Amazon

27355237R00044